DECADES

Under the Same Shared Sun

MARLANA DeMARCO HOGAN

NEWMAN SPRINGS PUBLISHING
320 Broad Street
Red Bank, NJ 07701

First originally published by Newman Springs Publishing 2024

ISBN 979-8-89061-803-0 (Paperback)
ISBN 979-8-89061-804-7 (Digital)

Printed in the United States of America

To my husband who has given me my
most treasured gift, our son.

PAN AMERICAN

Hand Me That Bootstrap

So you say we should come
To that new place that shares the same rising sun.
All else, you say, will be different and new—
Especially waiting just for you two.

We'll take that chance
Without even a glance.
We'll begin our new way
And there, we will start a new day.

Made in Italy

What was it like
Arriving on that flight,
With your family expanding
Surely not the best planning.

A little one on the way,
Wondering what your mother will say.
Such a difficult transition,
What were you both thinking?

As we would see
You two felt ready and free,
To step into a new life
Finding extra strength as husband and wife.

Their Big Mistake

I'm only here, thanks to Sister Dear
Who became deathly ill during a family duty fulfilled.

Mother was in Rome
To help her recently widowed brother left alone.

In tote were her two little ones
A baby girl and a son.

There to care for his young two
As if at just twenty years old she should know what to do.

When her youngest got sick,
There was barely time to think.

Her husband arrived.
The baby survived.

This young growing family was revived
And later, on to America they would thrive.

Birthright Citizenship
(The Stowaway)

Unintended pregnancy
Begins a new legacy.

First to gain citizenship,
A stowaway on an emigrant family's trip.

Four Italian immigrants arrive on a flight.
One American citizen arrives soon after, during one long laborious night.

First to be born in a hospital bed.
First to be bottle fed.

The others four, Mother, Father and the older two, all worked very
    hard to be naturalized,
While the younger one and I seemed to have found the shortcut to
    the finish line, gaining birthright citizenship—and I won the
    first prize.

Ah, Raspberries!
(Why Are You Here?)

Why are you here and not that other somewhere?
Sort of like me, here from across the great sea.
The choice not your own, why weren't we just left in our original home?
Now here we are in this beautiful space, yet both so out of place.

Child's Play

Every day outside to play
Running around the block.
Every day outside to play
Always racing the clock.

Every night inside just right
Sit down for something to eat.
Every night inside just right
TV is such a treat.

Brothers, Sister, Cousins, Friends

Brothers, sister, cousins, and friends
Let's begin by counting backward from ten.
Close your eyes, there will be no cheating or lies
Run and hide as we play for hours and hours outside.
Ringolevio, Truth or Dare
Playing all day without a care.

Cross the Creek to the Fort

Jump, stop, take a look up
Remember to watch your feet
Look all around, so many incredible sounds
As the water runs down the creek.

Across the creek where all the children meet
Neighborhood girls and neighborhood boys
All hands in the sand with feet on dry land
As we develop the day's construction plan.

Build a permanent wall that will ultimately fall
Dig a great canal with your favorite pal
Make some mud pies for those hunger cries
Get on your way at the end of a long play-filled day.

Slaughterhouse at Age Five

The effects never questioned
The lifelong results unpredicted, hardly mentioned

Quantity and quality at warehouse prices
Together with slaughterhouse vices

The abundance only appreciated
In this land of hope and opportunity

Once Upon Another Time
(Here's to You, My Mrs. Robinson)

From kindergarten to the third grade
Hazlet School, we had it made.
Tall windows, two floors, and a big playground
You had it all, hands down.

Mrs. Robinson with your bun
Mrs. Lawson's peanut brittle, yum
Every morning over the bridge
To school I would run, so fun.

La Luce del Sole

La luce del sole
La luce del sole
La luce del sole ti aiuterà.
A Mamma,
La luce del sole é
La luce di Dio.
La luce del sole ti aiuterà.

Growing Up in the Brainiac Zone

I remember the night
Oh what a fright
The parents already in bed,
Both exhausted, expecting the same old jam-packed day coming up
    straight ahead.

We four kids at the kitchen table,
Each developing our own particular brainiac label,
Focused diligently on our school work of the day
With an occasional shared laugh, elbow jab, or angry smirk after too
    much annoying play.

Then out from above
Came a loud howl filled with love—
Get to bed, now, off you go
Or all those books out the window I will throw.

As we quickly packed up our bags,
We all burst out into laughs
And we made our way up to our beds
With the greatest excuse for unfinished homework racing through
    our heads.

The Bedroom Next Door

Those very special people alone at last
Recollecting the very recent past.
Listening to the whispering of their voices
Along with the house's creaking, sleeping noises.

At times they would argue
Other times laughter
Until I'd fall asleep
And hear nothing else after.

Teacher Teacher

Teacher, teacher
Who are you?
Teacher, teacher
What do you do?

Teacher, teacher
You're young, you are old.
Teacher, teacher
You are weak, you are bold.

Teacher, teacher
Every day you are there.
Teacher, teacher
It matters that you care.

Teacher, teacher
We listen to what you say
Teacher, teacher
You affect us in every way.

Crazy World

Crazy walk
Crazy talk
Crazy dumb

Crazy girl
Crazy for boys
Having crazy fun

Yvonne, Patty, and Me

Yvonne, Patty, and me
Together, we three
Our adventure together
Our plan never better

Out all night
We stayed out of sight
We had our fun
And back with the sun

Yet little did we know
The search was on the go
Police and family out all night
We three together assumed all was right

The plan had a crack
Tears greeted us when we arrived back
Two punished the traditional way
Mine was worse, they didn't even have to say

Riding the Wave without a Clue

Riding the wave without a clue
A young girl misreading most cultural cues.
What was fought for, taken as her gain
From higher education to playing in a high school soccer game.

Riding the wave without a clue.
Entering a new world and a new age too.
Many challenging paths with plenty of bold steps
Unexpected clashes, crashes without hitting the breaks.

Riding the wave without a clue
Drowning in choices
Still hardly knowing what to do.

Title IX
(Growing Up Girl in America)

Who knew the effects of you
Who knew once there wasn't a you
Who knew I stepped right in to you
Who knew I was the lesser of the two

I knew something wasn't right
I knew there was a continued fight
I knew with every new day and night
We all moved closer to that big beautiful bright white light

Before, I was offered with a dowry
Before, I was made to marry
Before, I was property nothing more
Before, I was the worth of the male children that I bore

Now I can boldly step out
Now I can scream and shout
Now I can inherit my fair share
Now I can outwardly dare and not care if they stare

Survival of the Fittest

Survival of the fittest
Its meaning is clear.
Survival of the fittest
Makes me tremble with fear.

The fittest
So strong.
The fittest
So wrong.

Survival of the fittest
The idea in itself is troubling after all.
Survival of the fittest
A strange invincible creature in us all.

The fittest
Has evolved.
The fittest
Problem solved.

The Rat Race

Get on a bike
Harness the power
Get your workout
Paid by the hour

Take the steps
Put in the time
Transfer your energy
For a better world, yours and mine

Lose the weight
Keep the lights on
Walk it off
Take a run

Thanks to the rat race
Energy crisis, gone

Screens

Screens, you've opened up our lives
Screens, you help us to survive
Screens, you've brought in the sounds of the outdoors
Screens, you help us dry our floors

Screens, you help keep the bugs in their own space
Otherwise, they would overrun the place

Screams and Dreams

Dreams, you let in the absurd
Dreams, you modify each and every word
Dreams, you are in total control
Dreams, you give each of us the lead role

Dreams, you don't always end well
Dreams, hopefully the only place we may experience hell

God Got Me Good

My reason, sometimes unclear
My reason is not fear

Focused on the right thing
Not for what it might bring

Listen more than speak
The opposite is truly weak

Be fair and willing to share
Only because I care

Kindness is my shield
And with it, strength I do wield

Kill Them with Kindness (Three Cognates—*Rispetto/ Pazienza/Attenzione*)

Kill them with kindness
Not the best phrase
Kill them with kindness
How I filled my teacher days

Along with textbook
And highly valued piece of chalk
Respect, patience, and my undivided attention
Were the teacher tools I brought

Between Two Bells

I remember every day in this very way
Start with a smile as you all file in, not just my style
I actually couldn't get rid of that happy-to-see-you-all-again grin
Whether you smiled back or not, you knew it wasn't some sinister plot
You knew I did care and would always try to be fair

We'd start our little lesson at the sound of the bell
The one I worked on for hours and hours (I'm sure you could tell!)
Some of you tired, hungry, and sometimes bored, yes that I could see
You see, you couldn't get much passed me

We'd work our way through, as I listened attentively to each and
     every one of you
Those objectives would bring out the interest, the excitement in so
     many, it's true.

The classroom was too small, it could hardly fit us all
Or was it the thirty-plus students crammed in like a large horse stall
Often losing five minutes, just to get through a simple roll call
But little old me brought enough patience for us all

And as I made my way up and down each row
(Often bumping into a desk or two along with stubbing my big toe.)
Listening to all your sweet voices, I always hoped it was clear
Caring was the essence of each lesson
Presented daily, humbly, to every one of you, my students, held so dear

Obviously Elementary

When golfing one day
While learning how to play
I heard a cranky old White man say—
Obviously elementary

When golfing one day
Young and ready to play
I heard a cranky old White man say—
Obviously elementary

When golfing one day
As a female at play
I heard a cranky old White man say—
Obviously elementary

When golfing one day
A break from teaching to play
I heard a cranky old White man say—
Obviously elementary

Lady Liberty

How many times have I visited you?
How many school children have I brought up, down, and through?
How many visiting extended family members too?
Too many to count and all to see and experience much more than a
     statue as beautiful as you.

The Great American Blender

The great American blunder
So many different people
Living above and under
Right next to one another

The mixing of the races
So many different faces
Finding minimal traces
Of cultures lost, at what cost?

Shake it up to see
Wondering what we will be
The sum of you and me
Is it coffee or tea?

Maybe a blend
Try it with a friend
Add a bit of lemon
And make it sugar free.

Shake Up That Gene Pool

Shake up that gene pool
I always knew it was true
To develop a better me, you, and you.
Get out of that town
Get around, around, and around.

Shake up that gene pool
I always knew it was true
Too close together, too close to call.
Too close together, too close for us all.
If we stay we will all fall.

La Famiglia

Family first.
Family strong.
Family right.
Family wrong.
Trips to Italy, always an adventure.
Meeting and greeting
And some very good eating.
Look-alikes, similar names
L'Americana, L'Italiano
She looks like me, how could this be?
It's family, obviously.

Policastro

Policastro, quel giorno un disastro.
Esterina, quella bellina.
Persa nella confusione della giornata.
Sotto il sole sulla spiaggia.
Trovata dopo un'eternità.
Tante preghiere, una folla insieme.
Dieci minuti, un'eternità.

Rutgers, Do You Remember Me?

Rutgers, do you remember me?
You churned us out
Like a slaughterhouse
Processed meat, packaged so neat.

And yet I enjoyed my college days
While studying, it's true
But others, I know, faced so much trouble from you.

You Have No Idea

To bleed without a wound.
To bleed from inside the womb.
Three thousand, five hundred of my days.
Three thousand, five hundred different ways.

Could this be the fate for those like me?
And it only gets worse,
If there is a nine-month break from that curse.

Amazing Place

Conceived with medical assistance
Born with much resistance
Amazed how life begins
Yet I could never go through that again
Even with so much social insistence
Just feeling lucky to still be in existence.

Who Are You

Italian, that is true
Fifty percent from me to you

Irish, it's in your name
And so much more
From within your father's family picture—framed

Tyrolean, from northern Italy
Greek, Grams' husband, Red
The one we never met

And Native American Indian
They, too, are your kin
All inside you, deep within

The Natural-List

You loved to draw from the very start
Your sunburst to me is a work of art.
So many sketches and even more lists
As you chronicled your surroundings
Such a budding naturalist.

Outside you would play.
Outside you would stay.
With notebook and pencil in hand
Identifying the many living creatures of the land.

From one day to the next
One sighting would change to two
And later reporting all your daily observations
Was the ultimate, just what you loved to do.

Nine chipmunks, then ten
Two deer, no three!
So many different types of birds you would see.
And included on your list, naturally,
The neighbor's dog, Max, also nature-watching attentively.

Deer Ticks

Dear Ticks
Please let us back in

Dear Ticks
Okay, you win

Dear Ticks
We promise to be good

Dear Ticks
And from now on always care for the woods

Stingray Day Down at the Shore—A School's Class Trip

Pile in the car
And close the door
It's stingray day
Down at the shore.
Let's put down the blanket
Dip our feet in the waves
I could sit here for hours
And even for days.
A fading memory now
A foggy sight we did see
Many people were standing
We wondered what it could be.
Along the shore to the north we watched for a bit
It seemed to be snaking toward us
This wave of people standing tall, then they would suddenly sit.

It was in the water, we would see
As the show got closer to you and me
Hundreds of stingrays swimming by
As if smiling at us and waving—just saying hi.
It was a school of fish on a seaside swim
The ocean being their school's metaphorical gym.
And as each wave crashed, we all waved back.
It almost felt like an allied shoreline attack.
Together we took our turn and stood tall
To be absolutely sure to see it all
Then we quickly sat back down
As if nothing ever happened at all.
Relaxed and at ease, our eyes fixed on the seas
Again digging our feet in the sand…
Just added another magic moment
To the many memories from this exotic land.

Inchworm Inchworm

Inchworm, inchworm
Floating down from the sky
Inchworm, inchworm
Tethered from on high

On the way down
You sway your way to the ground
With the breeze
With such ease

Inchworm, Inchworm
Descending from the trees

Springalingaling
(Wakey, Wakey)

Wake up bees, wake up trees
Wake up birds and squirrels.
The sun is up, up high in the sky
Smiling down on all you boys and girls.
Springalingaling
Springalingaling
Springalingalingaling
Springalingaling
Springalingaling
Springalingalinglingling.

The Reading Tree
(Ancient Tulip Tree to You and Me)

Summertime
So much fun
Drop the electronics
Get out in the sun

Pick up a book
Find a quiet nook
In the shade under a tree
The number one place to be

When the Army Worms Arrived

I remember the day I looked up at our back wall
While working in the yard, I couldn't believe what I saw.
Black worms everywhere, how slow they would crawl.
Touch them, I wouldn't dare. It seemed from the air they did fall.
And there they would stay for many a day.
They adjusted to their new surroundings in their own special way.
It was during a big storm from the Gulf of Mexico, I read
They rode those rain clouds like a big ocean wave
And landed here in my backyard
All at once, as if an army did invade.

Tic-Tac-Snow

Tic-Tac-Toe in the snow
The thoughtful placement of the X or the O
The final line marks three in a row

Quickly cheer or present the regrettable—Oh no!
Then move on to draw the next blank board and see how long we
    can go…
The original Etch A Sketch using the earth and the snow

The Trees That Shouldn't Be

I watched you grow
Through many summers and snow.
I shed a tear
Every time I came near.
So sad for the reason
You brought beauty to each season.

Now you must go
To memorialize each and every lost soul.
Be on your way
Because there is so much you will help to say.

The Local Family Farm

Four-season farming
The ultimate goal
Four-season farming
No GMOs
Four-season farming
A bountiful harvest every week
Four-season farming
Delicious vegetables to eat
Four-season farming
Healthy food locally grown
Four-season farming
Support the source and bring some home

Ember Pember

Ember Pember
Good morning, good day
Ember Pember
Let's, together, get on our way.

Ember Pember
Time to open the coop
Ember Pember
Just give me a minute to pull up my boot.

Ember Pember
Go. Run. Play.
Ember Pember
Let's, together, enjoy another day.

Green Legs

Green Legs, you are one of a kind.
Green Legs, a mystery to the mind.
Green Legs, the color gave us a clue.
Green Legs, every day what you do.
Green Legs, your eggs, who knew!

Hello, Baby Chick

Hello, my little Baby Chick
So good to see you
Hello, my little Baby Chick
Love you through and through.

Hello, my little Baby Chick
Sit with me right here
Hello, my little Baby Chick
Love to have you near.

Hello, my little Baby Chick
You touched my heart from the start
Hello, my little Baby Chick
You are a true work of art.

Free at Fifty-three

Why not celebrate
Isn't it great

After so many years
Gone are the aches, pains, and fears

Of this, society doesn't speak
Yet affecting half the population so wore out and weak

Stand up, stay strong
You've got the rest of your life now to right the wrong

Encourage the rest
Give it your best

So Long

Women, when they broke your feet
They had you beat

Then they took your name
While threatening to bring you down in shame

You were handed a permanent over-the-shoulder purse
Weighted down and anchored, nothing could be worse

A painted face like a clown
Still unable to hide the invisible frown

Nails grown so long
The whole picture so wrong

On a First Name Basis

You were right, what you said that night
I need no title, or an added name
Given together in a wedding picture frame

And let's drop that paternal last name
It's all part of the same stifling life game

We've all been given a numerical code
To take us through life's long bumpy road

Let's leave it at that
Just put it under your proverbial hat

It's yours 'til death do you part
And, unable to break your heart

A unique identity for each and for all
Equally maintained through life
Wouldn't that be all right? That's all

A first name is more than enough
Or else show the true trail of maiden names
Would that be too rough?

It's what we've been carrying, covered by all that other stuff
We are not one name, but at least four
List them all, every time, or better yet with the many, many more

Following me is a history
A trail of names, but as a woman
The trail is lost, at such great cost

In the nuclear home, we are never alone, but as we spread out
The male names, so strong, seem to be the only ones carried on

The female is rebranded, renamed
Such an obvious identity loss and perpetual debilitating game

Original background now hidden
And so much more lost or forbidden

Growing up with one single last name
With that one dropped for the man you were looking for
Once married, why not carry and reveal at least your very own last four?

But, really, why—each are still paternal, spiraling back no matter
        how far we go
So what is the use? I really don't know

At birth we are proudly given the latest male's last name brand
And it, too, is to be erased once married
Like a strong wave hitting the shoreline covered with the day's long
        history temporarily imprinted in the sand

Lost at such a great cost
Soon to reveal, there is nothing left to steal

Instead, let's go ahead
First name and number, unique like no other

Father and Daughter Enterprises (Where You Are?)

On our daily call
We'd cover it all

Would you both come to me
Or maybe wait and see

Will we dig that ditch
Or fix the Barnegat switch

Pay some bills
Or review the wills

Finally decide what to eat
To make our day complete.

Mother and Son Enterprises

Now it's you and me
Not the tripod of three

No call to them
Just make a list with my pen

We'll go forward with each endeavor
Conquer the many tasks together

Cook up something good to eat
Then our day will be complete

Broken

I am broken.
Brokenhearted
Broken spirit
Broken boned
How I fear it.

Completed Tasks

He is with us no more like so many before
Through life and death, he did his best.
Hard worker, dedicated family man
Always focused on the completion of his simple daily plan.

He lived his life to the fullest
He taught by example
And through his eighty-seven years
We are fortunate to have received a full sample.

Almost Everything

As I stare at your chair and you're not there
I want to thank you for almost everything
You gave us your love
You gave us your blood
You gave us almost everything
As we gather to share and you're not there
I want to thank you for almost everything
You gave us your heart
But that was just the start
When I see you next
I want the rest

I Forgot It Could Rain

In the quiet night with no one in sight
The tears began to flow.
My cries were soft so blending with the creaking
Sleeping noises of your home.
Still unable to believe you left us all here alone.
Then came the added sound with no one else around.
The tears from above came pouring down
Unrecognizable to me because just for a moment, I forgot
How hard it could rain.

How Was I to Know?

Devoted daughter to the last day
Yet on that last day I said, "No, Dad."
I didn't want to go, Dad,
And it ended up to be your last day.
But how was I to know?
Oh, I miss you so.
And to you, Mom, I would always go
Yet on that last night, Mom
I didn't want to know,
Though you were struggling so.
But how was I to know
It would be your last day?
I am sorry is all that I can say.
Devoted daughter, except for that last day.

And Then There Were Ten

A family of six
A rooster and a hen
With four baby chicks
We filled a small den.

Then one with his mate
Had two little eggs
And I brought in one more
With my own rooster friend.

Another found a partner
And the last one hadn't yet.
Then from twelve, a full dozen
We went to ten, with great regret.

The Last Name Game

Born with, then removed
Identity you will lose
What was yours, lost for another
It happened the same way
To your very own mother

I Remember You

I remember you
I remember you
I remember you
Do you remember me?
I remember you

Coffee Time Cometh

When I was young, bright and early I would run
Up with the coffee to start the fun
Stir the two of them up with the morning sun.

Once a mom, after work I would run
Out with my coffee to wait for my son
Drink it up and finish the day, part one.

Now my coffee time is on hold
I sit and wait while it gets cold
As my weary bones grow old.

Slow-Motion Minutes to a Fast-Forward Day

Is there a way to skip this day?
Go right to tomorrow, be on my way.
I want to, but how? Perhaps I will pray.
Or just close my eyes until it is tomorrow, today

Living in the Danger Zone

You found your path
You found your home
Along your troubled way.
All on your own
So alone, so alone.
Such isolation
In the danger zone.

Cocooned
(So You Mean You Are Human)

Cocooned for years
Lost without tears
Frozen in place and waiting for it to pass
Feeling out of sorts, expecting a huge crash
Still thinking it through
Still not knowing what to do
Finally ready to take a chance
Finally ready to take a swim in the metaphorical ocean's expanse.

Eastpointe

Where the woods and the water meet
Where the wind can carry you off your feet
Where the clouds reach down from on high
And the elevated earth forms a cradle in the sky.

Address, the Issue

Trevico, Avellino
How I wish you were *più vicino*
Still, close to the heart
But oh so far apart!

Maria Buff's
It was a bit rough
Two young families together
Life couldn't be better!

Stuyvesant Avenue
Look what they would do
Lots of room to grow
It even brought in some extra dough!

Craig Street
My favorite place
My favorite space
Jersey shore couldn't be beat!

Downing Hill Lane
A beautiful gain
Where family would gather
And live happily ever after!

Deer Trail Drive
In the woods we would thrive
Nature at our front door
Who could ask for anything more!

Shared Moments

There is a sound the water makes
There is a sound when the smallest wave breaks
The trickle
And as the water flows down the stream
With the sun's rays reflective gleam
The ripple

Such a quiet place
Such a great escape

A place to share with flying bugs and birds
Sunning snakes and frogs and crawling ants and plants

All alone
And so at home
Staring at a curious chipmunk in this luscious nature zone

When the soft morning sun reaches down from above
I am led to this space that I truly love
Where backyard woods and ponded waters meet
Where the breeze sways the trees as I watch from my park benched seat

The freshness of the air
I wish always to share
The sweetness of the floral scents
Surround me along with a magnificent wooded fence

Each day begins with such beauty
Devising a way to forever share these moments is my duty

Owlie

I came upon a dying owl the other day.
At the end, she had only two final words to say.
As I approached, her eyes did open so wide.
Expecting to be trampled but with no strength to fly or
even try to hide.

Her wing was stuck in an awkward way
"I want to help you" was all I could manage to say.
With help and some leather gloves we did dare
I hoped she knew I really did care.

I sat alone with her for a while
She seemed frozen, paralyzed, unable to smile.
I spoke to her in a whispered voice
She closed her eyes, she had no choice.

I ran for water to give her some strength
I poured some on her beak, but she didn't seem to know
what it meant.
And as she struggled, moving each wing,
Her final *hoot*, *hoot* she did softly sing.

Modern Weekly Harvest

To the grocery store, what a bore
Not for me, try it my way, you will see

Up and down each isle, that is my style
Get in the zone, bring only what you need home

Never miss a sale, and remember
Don't forget the kale

Once a week, that's what I seek
Plan your daily meals, but only buy for the deals

Abundance all year long
Local and long-distance farming and factories try to stay strong

No need to worry about the season
Appreciate the work behind the price, there is a reason

Never break a nail or break a sweat
The modern-day harvest is a sure bet

The Neighborhood Cat (A Cat's Tale)

We do it a little differently here.
No rule, routine, or schedule to adhere.
Only the uneaten scraps thrown deep into the woods.
The crumbs and leftovers devoured before natural decomposing could
    even occur.
To many outdoor critters big and small,
The fox, the squirrels, the deer,
Perhaps even the big bad bear we all deeply fear,
And of course the stray cats held so dear,
A spectacular treat for them all.

The Kitty Cat Collection Agency I

No, I don't agree
This is not for me
I go about this so reluctantly.

You arrived one day
What could I say
When you decided to stay.

It was not soon after
With a bit of a chuckle, almost laughter
You returned with another, maybe your brother.

Today it's three
Who knows how many there will ultimately be
Let's just sit back, wait, and see.

Kitty Cat Collection Agency II

The cat lady I am not
But the day you arrived at my door
I knew I was in for a whole lot more
I fed you some fish
Must have been a favorite dish
You returned the next day
And seemed to have so much to say
A routine did begin
Until the day you arrived with him
Brother or son, I'm not sure which one
The only thing that was clear
You held him so dear
We started again
Figuring out how much and when
Then as we worked through a new schedule
Number three did appear
And brought confusion and fear
To the little boy cat, it was clear
Just as we begin to figure things out
It won't be long till number four cat, then five
Soon will stop by to say hi, oh my!
Find me that cat lady hat
I'm sure it will fit just fine.

Baby Talk, Big Boy Walk

Goo-goo gaa-gaa
The typical baby talk sounds
Until Wawa came around

And when there suddenly arrived a Google
Followed by so many more with babble-like names
I knew things would never be the same

The Wannabe, Me

I wanna have faith
I wanna have fun
I wanna be a vegetarian
I wanna enjoy the sun

Perky Percocet

It could have been me
Taken initially for my injured knee
Perpetual perky
Available at your local pharmacy
Perpetual perky
Available at a limited quantity
Perpetual perky
It will be the death of you and almost me.

One a Day

One a day
No way.
Three this week
Get off your seat.

Get outside
Walk, run,
Or just drive
And remember, stay alive.

My Race with Time—Sandy Hook
Beach, the Starting Line

I have a plan
Bring my own coffee
And work on my tan.

From the Sandy Hook
To the end of time
Pen to paper to share each new worded rhyme.

From beach to beach
And day by day
At the edge of the earth
A grown woman at play.

With each morning's sunrise
With both feet in the sand
I am plugged into the source
Gaining strength from this porous land.

Forever Ago

Forever ago.
Only a few weeks or so.
How long, I really don't know.
Forever ago.
We were all on the go.
Now home with our shared Internet, exchanging the occasional hello.
Forever ago.
It all seemed lightning fast, but no. This monster we hide from creeps oh so very slow.
Forever ago.
We truly didn't know.
Now so much we must leave behind, just simply let go.

The Coronavirus Crash
(Alone Together)

The coronavirus crash
It's been a mad dash.
To get to your spot
And finally stop.
Running all around,
All around countries and towns.
A worldwide game of musical chairs.
While exchanging helpless, questioning stares.
Get yourself together.
This won't be forever.
Remember it's now or never.
But when the music stops
Will it be me or you that drops?
Well, I hope not.

Census 2020
(Old Time Head Count Method)

Everyone back to where you are supposed to be.
Everyone, except you, you, and me.
Stay at home, remain alone.
Keep your distance, stay in place.
Everyone remain in your own particular space.
Unusual times, no reason or rhyme.
Watch the pandemic graph map with numbers that continue to climb.
World picture, all in place.
Most people have returned to home base.
Census count accurate across the globe.
Snapshot of the earth's population accurately told.

The Air We Share
(A Coronavirus Connection)

Let's share some air.
Let them stare.
I don't care.
Do you dare?
Imagine, you and me, a deadly pair.

Also titled, "Love Universal COVID-19 Style"

With Appreciation

As we ran out, you hurried in.
Battling another fire…
Knowing you don't always win.

Ode to the Purple Porta Potty

Oh how straight and tall you stand.
A beacon in a long deserted land.
There you will remain
Until the power is restored once again.

The Bewitching Hour

Remember the green glow
Oh no!
And now the sooty smell
Oh well…

Spindles and Windows

Remaking our home.
Never felt more alone.
Lots went up in smoke
Memories of all the old folk.
It was horrible, no joke.
Construction goes on.
So much money and time.
Thank goodness for insurance.
Still, a marathon of endurance.
And with added money of our own
We helped spruce up the house's old bones.

The Home Stretch

Today for the first time I couldn't stay.
I don't know why, I couldn't even try.
So much, only partially done.
So frustrated, I just had to run.
Then what did I do,
Other than thinking of you, you, and you?
I made the last jar of pasta sauce.
And added those remaining few amazing mushrooms, sauteed, of course.
It wasn't many hours after the shake.
A very rare 3.1 NJ earthquake.
The one that hit right under our feet.
The one that hit while still displaced during another long restless
    night's sleep.
When I awoke at exactly 2:00 a.m. and heard a horrible boom,
I knew I was in trouble again.

My Imaginary Us

The path to the pond
When it's morning time
It's mine, all mine.

Up and down
Around and around
Without a sound

The sun in my eyes
No need to deny

An imaginary us
And my lifelong crush.

A Way of Life

Life takes us away
Life makes us stay
Life often gets in the way
Day after day after day.

I Want to Write

I want to write
Here, there, and everywhere.
I'm done here.
Let's go there,
Without a care.

Husband and Son

Husband and son
Husband and son
Together again
Together as one

Devotion

To my mother and father
And another one
To my son, my son
The only other one

Between You and Me

Between you and me
There is now a continent
And the sea.
Between you and me
An umbilical cord was cut
To set you free.
Between you and me
There is a long history.
Between you and me.
Between you and me
A dear love will always be.
Between you and me.

A Pause with Awe
(Original Title: "Applause with Awe")

As I looked up to the south with the sun rising from the east,
I wondered what that flickering in those trees could be.
It was shadows from up above in the leaves of the trees,
And then, suddenly, from behind, you and your flock flew right over me.
You quickly passed me, a little squirrel, and a few other creatures of
    this crazy amazing world.
And all at once, one by one, you plunged directly into the pond right
    in front of us all as we paused just for a moment and watched
    with amazement and awe.

Duckweed

Duckweed, you're our future side dish
Duckweed, you give shelter to all the little fish
Duckweed, we should harvest you each season
Duckweed, you feed the geese and ducks that don't seem to be leaving

The Squirrel's Nest—Me and the Trees, We're Up Here

My little nest
Has just been refreshed.
Inspections. Approved.
I'm back in the groove.
All on my own
Home sweet home.

The Thin Place

My thin place
My small space
More than enough
At times even too rough.

Once a Pond in Time/Once Upon a Pond

Mud puddle
Mud puddle
What have you done?

Mud puddle
Mud puddle
The pond is almost gone

Less water
More ground
Grass sprouting all around

A Pond No More

A pond no more
The place I adore
A mud puddle is all
Yet as alluring as before

To the birds and the bees
To the flowers and the trees
And of course to you and me.

Missed

You missed the spring,
The birds again started to sing.

You missed the blooming flowers,
Always their greatest hour.

Untitled

Out from the open
Unseen and unknown
Surrounded by many
Completely alone

You Two Made This
(To Mend from Within)

You brought me here—
I would scream
At the peak of my teenage years.

Tears and fears from a mom,
I would see
Sitting on that top step, so late, just waiting for me.

Now mine is the fear
For someone so dear.
He blames us for this
But how is it fixed?

We put him here on this earth.
He seems unclear of his self-worth.
Broken and lost,
The road to mend has a great cost.

With Hope, There Is That Possibility

Thank you all,
Too many names to absorb.
One, two, and three
And yes, so many, many more.

You all take their care
Run here, there, and there
And work to bring our loved ones back, we pray
Hoping for that better day
Back to as many of those waiting, including me
As many as there can possibly be.

A-mom-ynous

When Time Is a Monster: The Struggles from Within

After more than a decade
Of watching friendships slowly fade
Isolation and separation
A true struggle from within

This slow-motion crisis
With a dramatic yet predictable end
The help reluctantly welcomed
Please allow a good life to finally begin again

A Day without Laughter
(Time Is a Monster)

Looking forward to that day
Looking back he would say—
What is happening to me and why?
Pseudobulbar what a name
Pseudobulbar what a game
Laughter without fun
Feels like a day without the sun
A genetic weakness triggered by life
Or a traumatic brain injury that cuts like a knife
Whatever the cause
Life now is on pause
Getting through each day
In the most unusual way
Isolation, his only friend
Isolation, if time he could bend
But for now time is monstrous
Until the end of this laughter, so preposterous

Cause and Effect

Cause and effect
So difficult to detect

Was it those things I did
That altered my id

Was it those family traits
That I've grown to hate

Was it those trees and the breeze
Resulting in more than a sneeze

A combination perhaps
Please, not another relapse

Dear Ticks (Part II)

How could it be
You've stolen him from me

What have you gained
From his suffering and daily chronic pain

Your bite
Must have been just right

Weird Winds

This theory I've contrived
Effects caused by planes in the skies

Pushing the air as they go
Ripples of wind begin to flow

Not unlike the fish in the water
With every move, their environment altered

We now streak, back and forth
Rockets added at such great force

Waves of wind begin to grow
Permanently affecting the natural flow

The beginning of the end for you and me
Soon to be obvious for all to see

Early Arrivals
(Garage Cat and the Visiting Geese)

Up walked the cat
Tired as could be
The sun was just rising
She was ready for a good long sleep

Down came the geese
They screeched a firm landing
And as they strolled around the pond
They ate up the grass like it was melt-in-your-mouth green cotton
    candy

So Creepy

The age of connectivity
So creepy, actually.
The age of virtual activity
So creepy and so not for me.

Coronavirus Bump

Lucky it's been
With each purchase a win.
Up to this last condo sale
I've had a financially successful transactional trail.

It's Beginning to Look a Lot Like Sixty

It's beginning to look a lot like sixty
Each and every day.
From the arthritis in my knees
To the daily loss of my stinking keys,
Sixty, hello.

It's beginning to look a lot like sixty.
Everywhere I look.
So many wrinkles on my face
So many more inches around my waist.
Sixty, oh no.

Status Free in 2023—
Unranked and Unraveled

Don't put me on a list
Just give me a kiss

Don't get pictured with a famous other
Just hug your own mother

Don't treasure the who you met
Just live your life without regret

I Won't Go without You...

I wouldn't go when you, you, or you were hurting so
Precious family days lost, came at a great cost

So how could I enter and participate
If you, you, or you are left behind at that heavenly gate

But let's get one thing straight
For me please don't wait

Where to Be

Where to be
It's here for me
Surrounded by trees
And not far from the sea.

Ideal, Not Perfect

The view from the sand,
Isn't life grand?
The best from across the land,
And so soft in my hand.

Hugging the Coast

Hugging the coast.
Love it the most.
Loving the sea.
So close to me.
The salt in the air.
The sand in my hair.
The drive, the walk, the run.
The warmth beneath the sun.

Five Children's Books in
Search of a Display

Dragonfly Zone, no more are you alone.
Make room for the rest, here in our little nest.
Just a few more days and off you all will go,
Each with your own individual titles that will surely steal the show.
Each of you, take your turn. Each to reign for a day.
Four glorious days at the Bologna Children's Book Fair you will stay.
On the Sunday before, as a prelude for what is in store
Dragonfly my dearest,
Reign on that day, in your own special way.
Let each recite their story.
Let each feel the glory.
You take the lead and for all of you I will pray.
And remember, you each have something very special to say.

Piece Work

Piece work, it's all about putting the pieces together.
Piece work, it's all about keeping the pieces together.
Piece work, the work that we will later need to mend.
Peace work, the work that never ends.

A Toast to Many Good Tomorrows

The best day
It was yesterday
You really are back
You are on the right track

Today, we will see
If you feel ready and free
Good luck to you, you, and yes, even me

Morning, Cory

Good morning, Cory.
How are you?
What today
Do you plan to do?

Up and out
As you begin to shout.
So much on the list
That so many have missed.

Take your time
But hurry up.
Make things right
And then don't forget to turn out the light.

About the Author

On October 3, 1961, just three months after their arrival to the United States of America from Italy, Marlana, birth name Maria Vittoria Agnese and also known as Mariolina to family members, was born in Newark, New Jersey, to Antonio and Rosetta DeMarco, both from Trevico, Avellino. The third of four children, Marlana grew up in Hazlet, New Jersey, enjoying the warmth of a loving traditional Italian family. The years were filled with the seemingly endless opportunities and obstacles so many immigrant families face while searching for their very own version of the American dream.

Marlana graduated from Rutgers University in 1984, with a teaching degree in Italian language and culture. Her teaching career spanned twenty-five years in the Old Bridge Township Public School System, and she aimed to spread a love for lifelong learning to her many wonderful students.

After starting a family of her own in Millstone Township, she continued—often with her son, Barry, and dog, Ember—to explore all that New Jersey has to offer from the Jersey Shore to the ever-changing pond in their very own magical backyard. And together with extended family members, forever memories were made from the many treasured trips back to the medieval castle and family homesteads atop that small mountain town called Trevico, along the Apennines in Southern Italy. Heartfelt journeys summed up as a sentimental version of time travel. Experiential learning at its best for every historian at heart!